Contents

A Play

The Carnival Horse

Story by Wendy Graham

People in the Play

Narrator

Tommy

Mr Turner

Tommy's Mother

First Boy

Second Boy

Narrator

Tommy loved Bravo, the old horse
from the merry-go-round.
Bravo stood inside Mr Turner's shop.
He had been there for a long time.
His paint had once been white,
but now it was cracked and dirty.
His mane was thin and ragged
and his eyes looked grey and sad.

But Tommy thought Bravo was beautiful.

Mr Turner

Long ago, Bravo was a fine horse.
Look at this photo, Tommy.
Bravo was once the best horse
on the merry-go-round at a carnival.

Mr Turner

All the children wanted to ride Bravo.
But when the carnival closed down,
Bravo was brought here to my shop.
I put him on a stand near the doorway.
Each hoof was fixed to the stand with a strap.

Little children would climb onto his back.
They shouted with excitement
as they tried to make Bravo
move up and down.
But Bravo couldn't move any more.

Narrator

Tommy didn't mind. He hugged Bravo.

Tommy

You are still a great horse, Bravo.

Narrator

One day, when Tommy was in the shop with his mother, two older boys climbed onto Bravo's back.

First Boy

Come on, move, you silly old horse.

Narrator

The boy pulled hard on Bravo's mane.
Tommy rushed up to stop him.

Tommy

You are too big for that horse.
Get off and leave him alone.

Second Boy *(laughing)*

It's only an old bit of junk.

Narrator

Both boys jumped down and walked away.
Bravo wobbled on his stand.

Tommy *(in a soft voice)*

You are not a bit of junk.
But two of the straps
holding your hoofs have come off.

Narrator

As Tommy bent down
to have a closer look,
something terrible happened.

Narrator

Bravo fell right off the stand.

CRASH!

Bravo crashed to the floor.

Narrator

Mr Turner and Tommy's mother hurried over.

Tommy *(in a very sad voice)*

I'm sorry.

Narrator

Tommy tried to lift the horse up.

Mr Turner

It's all right, Tommy.
Those big boys
shouldn't have been riding Bravo.
Anyway, he's just a broken-down,
old carnival horse.
The rubbish tip is the place for him now.

Tommy's Mother

Oh! Bravo does have some big scratches
on his side.

Narrator

Mr Turner stood Bravo up against the wall.

Narrator

Bravo's sad, grey eyes
seemed to be staring at Tommy.

Tommy

Mr Turner,
please don't take him to the rubbish tip.
Mum, could I have him?

Tommy's Mother

Oh, Tommy. He's no use now.

Tommy

But I like him.
Please can we take him home?

Tommy's Mother *(smiling)*

All right, then. I can see you really want Bravo.

Narrator

When they got home,
Tommy's mother helped him
to fix the horse back on its stand.

Then, Tommy washed Bravo all over.

When Bravo was dry,
Tommy found some paint
and covered up every scratch.

Next, he brushed Bravo's mane and tail
and rubbed the saddle until it shone.

Tommy

You are my horse, now, Bravo.

Narrator

Then, Tommy noticed something.

Tommy *(happily)*

Oh, Bravo!

Your eyes aren't sad and grey any more.

They are bright blue and they are shining!

A Play

The Kindest Family

Story retold by Krista Bell

People in the Play

Narrator

Old Woman

Rich Lady

Mother

Family Members

Narrator

Once upon a time,
a poor family lived in a small village.
They had to work very hard
to grow enough rice to eat.
The family had hardly any money,
but they were always kind
to everyone.

Narrator

Up on a nearby hill,
there lived a rich lady.
She gave nothing to the poor family
who lived below her,
and she was unkind
to everyone in the village.

Narrator

One day, a very old woman came to the village.
She had ragged clothes
and she looked tired.
She walked slowly up the hill
to the rich lady's house,
and knocked on the door.

Knock, knock!

Old Woman *(in a tired voice)*

Could you give me something
to eat and drink, please?
I've come a long way
and I'm hungry.
I'm tired, too,
and I need somewhere to rest.
May I come in?

Rich Lady *(crossly)*

No, you may not!

You're too old and ragged

to come in here.

Go away and leave me alone!

Narrator

The old lady hobbled
down the road to the house
where the poor family lived.
She knocked on their door.
Knock, knock!

Old Woman *(in a tired voice)*

Could you give me something
to eat and drink, please?
I've come a long way
and I'm hungry.
I'm tired, too,
and I need somewhere to rest.
May I come in?

Mother

Yes, you may.
Come and have some of our rice.

Narrator

Everyone in the family was hungry,
but they gave the old woman
all that they had to eat
and all that they had to drink.

Mother

Would you like to have a rest now?
You can sleep on one of our beds.

Narrator

When the family woke up
the next morning,
they were surprised to see
that the old woman
was now dressed in fine clothes.
She was holding a golden sack.

Old Woman

I came to this village
hoping to find some kind people.
And you are the kindest family
I have ever met.
So, I'm going to give you this golden sack.
Just hold it open and say these words …

"Come! Come!

Fill up the sack!"

and it will fill with rice.

Narrator

Then, the old woman left the house
and disappeared down the road.

Narrator

The family was delighted.
They said the words
for the first time …

Family Members *(loudly)*

Come! Come!
Fill up the sack!

Narrator

At once, the sack filled with rice.

Narrator

Now, the poor family
had all the rice they wanted.
They gave some of it
to the other poor families
in the village.
They sold some of it
to the people who were able to buy it.

Soon, they had enough money
to buy anything they needed.

Narrator

The unkind lady who lived on the hill was very annoyed.

Rich Lady *(speaking to the mother in an angry voice)*

How did you become rich so quickly?

Mother *(smiling)*

Do you remember
the ragged old woman
who came to our village?
We were kind to her,
and she repaid us.

Rich Lady

I will never be unkind to anyone, again.

I have learned my lesson.

Narrator

From that day on,
everyone in the village
lived happily together.